Whar a candel will not burn...

Park Level Mine	3
1878 – a troubled year	4
Killhope in 1878	8
Health and safety at work	10
Craftsmen in stone	14
Deadwork	18
Timbermen	22
Stoping – the Heart of the Mine	24
The Black Spit	30
The Old Man	32
Managing the Mine	36
Park Level	40
The Engine Chamber	42
The last word	48

Park Level Mine

Park Level Mine was started in 1853.

The mine closed in 1910, was reopened briefly in 1916, and has never worked since then.

When in full production it produced 1000 tons of lead ore a year, and hundreds of men in Weardale found employment in it.

At its peak it was one of the richest lead mines in the whole British Isles, with well over a hundred men toiling underground.

At least two men died in the mine, several were injured by explosions, and an unknown number were sentenced to an early death through lung disease.

Park Level Mine was an ever present factor in the working lives of the families of the Killhope valley for half a century.

Now Park Level Mine's miles of tunnel are nearly all inaccessible, blocked with roof falls, flooded and silent.

Probably no-one will ever again see where Peter Milburn worked by candlelight week in, week out for a quarter of a century; the place where young Thomas Harrison lost his life after an explosion; where Titus Peart made a great deal of money in a rich vein of ore, or where Thomas Graham told his workmates about the latest letter from his brother Joseph in America.

A whole community of men worked down Park Level Mine. Skilled miners with years of experience and great knowledge of the signs of mining; younger men with enthusiasm and strength; craftsmen who laid the rail track, set the timber, and built the stone arching, agents and surveyors who made the decisions which affected the lives of all of them. Men who struggled to earn enough to feed themselves and their families.

Park Level Visitor Mine, within the Park Level Mine, shows something of the working lives of these men, and thousands more like them who worked in scores of lead mines beneath the bleak hillsides of the north Pennines to satisfy the demand of industrial Britain for lead.

Most of the Killhope men are now just shadowy figures from the past, and we have to use our imagination to flesh them out. This photograph of a Killhope miner gives us a glimpse of one of the real people whose story this book tells.

1878 A Troubled Year

1878 WAS A TURBULENT YEAR IN THE HISTORY OF PARK LEVEL MINE.

Lead ore (galena) is found in nearly vertical veins of mineral. For over twenty years the miners in Park Level Mine had burrowed further into the hillside, cutting and working 14 different veins of ore. They worked Old Moss Vein, Middle Grove Vein, Hazely Vein, Tweed and Trent Veins and many more. Some were good, some were bad, and some were indifferent. Mining was always a gamble. In 1874 rich deposits were found at Killhopehead Vein, a mile into the mine.

So much mineral came pouring out of this vein that WB Lead, the mine owners, built a brand new water powered crushing and separation plant – Park Level Mill. This started work in 1878.

Then the bottom dropped out of the lead market.

This had happened before, as the industry was notoriously prone to boom and bust – to periods of relative prosperity for the miners' families, followed by periods of severe hardship. The price of lead had always recovered, and men went back to work. This time the price didn't recover – too much lead was coming from foreign mines, at lower prices. Over a period of just a few years the north Pennine lead industry was more or less wiped out, apart from a few well organised, rich and profitable mines.

Mr. Beaumont. Owner of WB Mines. Always refused to say how much he earned from his mines, but supposed to be around £100,000 a year for many years.

...1878
A Troubled Year

For five years, Park Level Mine and its miners lurched from crisis to crisis, as WB Lead, owner of nearly all the dale's mines, struggled to cut their costs. For the miners of Weardale and their families this was a time of massive insecurity – and many left to start a new life elsewhere.

In 1883 Mr. Beaumont, who owned WB Lead, finally abandoned his Weardale mines. They had been in his family for over two hundred years.

A new company – the Weardale Lead Company – took over the mines – including Killhope. For another decade or more Killhope worked on, profitably, but with fewer miners. The best days were over.

Park Level Visitor Mine takes you back to the Killhope of 1878, to a time of deepening recession and insecurity. This book tells the story of Park Level Mine, and of some of the people who worked there.

PUDDING THORN
AUGUST 15 1878
Dear Brother I write these few lines to hear how you are getting on and how work is with you. The men on Killhope are all of (off) work but 6 partnerships and the Ironstone men has got their notice to leave their work. We are all of (off) work with the rest of men. but Thom he has got a job in Northumberland burning lime. We are all in good health around heare but Christopher Graham and he has worked none since November..... **FROM YOUR BROTHER THOMAS GRAHAM**

So wrote Thomas Graham, leadminer, to his brother Joseph who had emigrated to America a quarter of a century earlier.

Killhope
in 1878

Today Killhope seems remote, isolated and lonely. Only a handful of people live in the Killhope valley. Much of the land is farmed from a farm in Westgate, seven miles further down Weardale. A gamekeeper lives nearby, and many of the miners' cottages have been renovated as part of a grouse shooting estate.

In 1878 this valley was full of people, most with young families. At Park Level Mine and Mill (Killhope Lead Mining Centre) the stonework on the mine entrance and the stone slated mineshop next to it was mellowing. The washing rake was beginning to look a bit tatty with age and use. By contrast the buildings and woodwork of Park Level Mill were clean and new, the machinery fresh and modern.

Much of the bouse (the mixture of lead ore and waste produced by the miners from the veins) brought out for separation at the washing rake or mill came from far inside the mine. From Killhopehead vein the journey was a mile underground, with tubs filled from hoppers and then rumbling and clattering along the underground waggonway pulled by a sturdy dales pony. Other men's ore came from the low levels of Middle Grove vein. Small waggons were loaded by hand and pushed along the waggonway to the foot of the shaft. Here the bouse was tipped from the tubs to form a glistening heap which sparkled in the candlelight. Next it was loaded into kibbles (small buckets) to be hauled 120 feet (36.6 metres) up Vickers' Shaft by a rope wound round a simple roller. At the top of the shaft, bouse was loaded into the larger horse drawn waggons for the half mile trek along Park Level to the daylight.

Standing outside the mine you hear a distant rumbling approaching and soon see a dimly flickering light in the distance, swaying from side to side. As the light gets nearer it can be made out as a candle in a home made lantern hung from the neck of a horse. The pony bursts from the level pulling a rake of two tubs. An elderly, pale and thin man sitting on the first tub behind the pony climbs stiffly down, unhooks the trace chains, and the horse walks off to the left. The tubs roll gently on over the bouse teems. Once over the correct spot, the bottom of each tub is opened, and the bouse pours down into the storage bay beneath. From here it will be barrowed for washing at the washing rake or at the mill, and the lead ore taken out of it will journey on again, hauled by a traction engine, to the smelt mill at Allendale Town. Lead from the mill finds its way to Blaydon Wharf on the Tyne, and from there to market. It is a long journey from Cuthbert Peart's working in Middle Grove Vein to London.

Health & Safety

at Work

Methane or explosive gas is almost unheard of in lead mines. The men of 1878 did not need safety lamps, and often they smoked their clay pipes down the mine.

Visitors enter Park Level, the tunnel leading into the mine, as Thomas Graham, Peter Milburn and hundreds of other Weardale leadminers did before them.

But conditions now are very different.

In 1878 the miners had their own "grove clothes" for the mine. "Grove clothes" were ordinary clothes grown old and tatty and worn, but not yet quite ready to be cut up for rugs!

Men wore flannel underclothes, homemade flannel shirts, and fustian trousers, tied with a string below the knee for ease of movement. A waistcoat was common, and, for walking to work, a thick woven woollen plaid wrapped round the shoulders. Clogs were the universal footwear. Lighting was by candle, carried in a home-made wood and tin lantern, or perhaps stuck to a felt hat with a blob of clay.

There was no protective clothing provided, and no laws insisted on it. Nothing safeguarded the working conditions of the men. No-one checked whether the mine was safe before men began work, or whether the air in the mine was good. Very often it was not, and tales are told of miners having to whirl their coats round to get the air moving so that they could reach their place of work. Frequently there was so little oxygen that candles would only burn laid on their sides, with the fat or wax dripping into the flame.

Grove, or groove, is a very old dialect word for mine. It survives in a number of place names today.

Nobody now knows who these two men were. Probably they were Grahams, for this picture was found amongst Joseph Graham's family papers. Joseph emigrated from Killhope to America in 1852.

...Health & Safety
at work

In 1878 the first law made by parliament to cover lead mines was only six years old. The "Metalliferous Mines Regulation Act" was the first attempt to set minimum safety requirements.

Today the operation of Park Level Mine is covered by Her Majesty's Inspectorate of Mines, whose Inspectors have to approve everything we do. We have had to put steel supports in a section of the tunnel to meet modern standards.

The "grove clothes" of today include a hard hat, equipped with an electric light powered from a battery strapped round the waist.

A stream of water runs constantly down the mine tunnel, for this is a drainage level, draining water from workings deep in the hill. In 1878 miners walked in on the rail track, keeping their balance with the help of their walking sticks. They must, even so, have got wet feet at the beginning of their shift. Today's visitors wear overshoes or wellingtons to keep dry.

Ventilation is good in Park Level Mine today, with most of the workings blocked off.

Despite these modern comforts, Park Level Mine recreates the atmosphere of a nineteenth century lead mine, and shows what life was like for the men who worked in it.

Craftsmen
in stone

Park Level is an "adit" mine, driven as a tunnel big enough for dales ponies to walk in, and in a straight line towards where the veins are known to be.

Peter Milburn, Jos. Carrick, Jos. Emerson and Jos. Peart started cutting this tunnel in January 1853. The hillside they worked through is covered with stiff blue boulder clay, left after the ice age and full of large boulders. This is difficult ground to keep an open tunnel through, as it tries to squeeze passages shut.

The leadminers' answer was not to use timber supports, but, in the largely treeless North Pennines, dry stone arching to line the tunnel. Outside pressure on this arching merely binds it more strongly together. Peter Milburn and his fellow miners first cut the tunnel open, but it fell to specialist craftsmen to build the arching.

No-one now practices this craft, but the lead companies' stone masons, like Edward English, built miles and miles of beautifully constructed stone tunnels underground. Park Level Mine's stonework looks new – it is well over a hundred and thirty years old.

The labour that goes into stone arching is enormous. First the masons find a spot where suitable rock lies near the surface – preferably close to the mine. Then the labourers strip off the surface soil and broken rock, opening up the quarry. They quarry the rock, and the masons dress or shape it into suitable sized blocks on the surface. A good sandstone will split cleanly along flat bedding planes. Cartloads of stone are trundled to the mine, and transferred to mine tubs to be hauled into the mine where the stone is needed. After all this the masons begin the really skilled work, building up their arching on wooden formwork by the light of a couple of smoky tallow candles. Not a drop of cement or mortar is used anywhere.

EDWARD ENGLISH, STONEMASON Edward English was a stonemason all his working life. In 1878 he was an old man of 65, but still working. One of the specialist craftsmen employed by WB Lead, he worked both on the surface and underground, and many examples of his skill survive to this day. He built much of what you see on the surface at Killhope, including the jigger house, the bouse teems, and the washers' shop. He was usually paid by the yard of wall built. He did a lot of the underground arching in the Killhope mine. Edward lived at Burnt Hills, a mile or so down the valley from Killhope, where he had a small farm. Edward and his wife Mary had 9 children. Like many of the people in our story, some of his descendants still live locally.

...CRAFTSMEN IN STONE

Horse levels like this were common in the 19th century in the North Pennines. Although expensive to build they had two main advantages over shaft mines; the bouse could be pulled out easily with horses, and water drained from the workings along the level. Expensive pumps were not needed.

You can find beautiful stonework in mines today, as sound as when it was built. Particularly impressive are the junctions in levels, where the masons could really show off their skills. Stone arching is a wonderful feature of many North Pennine lead mines.

Icy cold water always flows out of Park Level in a constant stream. Some of it was used outside on the washing rake, and some was carried in a ditch to the next mine two miles downstream and used there.

Stone arching was cheaper and longer lasting than timber props. The London Lead Company did some calculations about the relative costs for their mines at Nenthead.

The Lead Company's Mines, Nenthead.

Cost etc. per fathom of timbering the mines:	
To 9 pieces of larch timber 6 feet long, each containing 1¼ cu ft, at 1/6 per foot	0/16/10½
To 12 pieces of larch timber 6 feet long, each containing 3 superficial feet at 1½d per foot	0/4/6
To carriage of timber into the mines, 6 waggons, at 4d per waggon	0/2/0
To fixing timber, 2 days at 3/- per day	0/6/0
To filling and drawing work produced in fixing timber, 3 waggons at 8d per waggon	0/2/0
	Total cost per fathom £1/13/4
Cost etc. per fathom of arching the mines:	
To winning and leading stones to the mines, 1 fathom at 8/- per fathom	0/8/0
To taking stones into the mines, 6 waggons, at 4d per waggon	0/2/0
To walling and arching levels, 1 fathom, at 11/- per fathom	0/11/0
To filling and drawing work produced in fixing arch, 3 waggons, at 8d per waggon	0/2/0
	Total cost per fathom £1/3/0

4th October 1862

(A FATHOM IS 6 FEET, OR 1.83 METRES)

Thos Peart 4 prs agree to drive as directed at 140/- per fathom and 20/- per bing. Thos Peart, John Peart (Adam's), John Hodgson, Thos Emerson (Mary's).

August 1878

Milburn's Level, driven in sandstone. A string has petered out after being followed from where it was cut in Park Level. Another string running off it leads into a vein.

Deadw

Lead mining was always a gamble. Just because miners knew where a vein was, didn't mean they knew whether it was productive or not. The only way of finding out was to get to the vein. Then as you followed it, it might "pinch out" to a mere string or thin line of unproductive mineral. Or it might improve to become a rich orebody. The miner's language was full of words describing a vein almost as if it was alive. She might "twitch" or "belly". Veins were always feminine. "Quick" veins carried ore, "dead" ones did not. Learning the signs and indications of what a vein might do was a lifetime's work. It is no coincidence that the science of geology grew out of the art of mining, and that the first geologists were practical miners who were trying to understand the three dimensional puzzle they were in. But mining remained a gamble. Like the lottery, the few really rich strikes seized the imagination of the whole district, and gave everyone hope that their turn would be next.

Taking a Bargain

Leadminers were paid only for the ore they produced. They worked in gangs or "partnerships" usually of four men. The price for their ore was fixed every three months – this was the "bargain". Regardless of whether the vein got richer or poorer, the bargain price remained the same for the whole three months. Miners were paid every six months, at the end of two bargains.

As long as they continued working, they got a weekly or monthly advance against their final pay. This lent money was raised to £2/10/0 (£2.50) a month after a strike in 1872. Before this it had stayed the same – £2 per month – for 25 years.

Although miners regarded themselves as free agents, conducting a negotiation or bargain with the mine management, and free to go to the mine when they chose, the mine owners insisted they worked 40 hours a week. Compared with many factory workers, miners worked quite short hours.

Thos. Peart and partners baiting away from the dust of their working.

...DEADWORK

JOHN PEART (ADAM'S) John
Peart was the most common name at the top end of Weardale in the last century. In the few miles of the valley west of Cowshill we can count 45 John Pearts in the 19th century census returns.

No wonder our John is identified by his father's name as well. Adam Peart and his family lived at Holywell, the small white house opposite the lead mining centre. His father was a miner and his five brothers were all miners. Like many, the family had a tiny farm which gave them fresh food and a little extra money. John Peart's mother, Jane, also brought in a bit of extra money by cleaning the office at Killhope. John Peart was 32 years old in 1878.

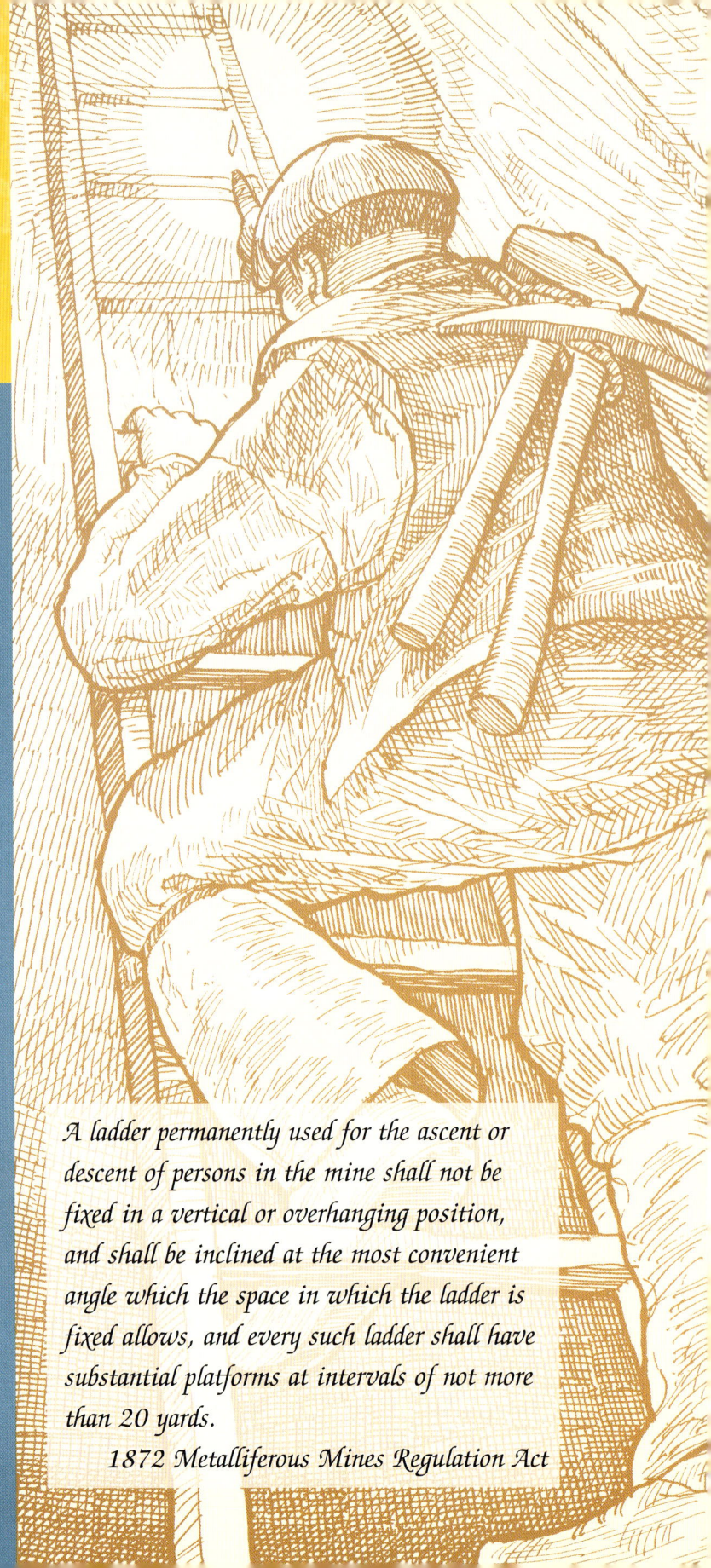

> A ladder permanently used for the ascent or descent of persons in the mine shall not be fixed in a vertical or overhanging position, and shall be inclined at the most convenient angle which the space in which the ladder is fixed allows, and every such ladder shall have substantial platforms at intervals of not more than 20 yards.
> 1872 Metalliferous Mines Regulation Act

A string of mineral crossing Park Level would be followed to see if it turned into a productive vein.

This work, like driving tunnels through unproductive rock, was called "deadwork", because it produced no ore. Miners on deadwork were paid by the fathom (six feet length or just under two metres) of rock they cut through.

In times of prosperity many men were set on deadwork to open up new areas of the mine, and to explore for new veins. In hard times deadwork was cut back. In August 1878, after a couple of months when nobody was at work, 41 miners were set to work in Park Level Mine. Only 12 of them were doing any deadwork.

Men on deadwork did more than drive the levels. They cut out the shafts in the mine – "rises" if they went upwards, "sumps" if they went down. Cutting a rise was very often unpleasantly wet work, with water pouring from fissures and cracks in the rock down onto the working men.

Rises and sumps connected the different levels in the mine and were used both for men to climb up and down, and to either drop bouse down or haul it up. A shaft used for both these things was called a "hopper and waygate". It was divided down the middle by a central "brattice" of timber, to keep the ladderway separate from the falling bouse.

Shafts were climbed sometimes by chain ladder, but more usually on "stemples" – short pieces of wood wedged across the corner of the shaft – or on ladders. Ladders and stagings were among the things kept in good order by the mine timbermen.

It costs money to haul deads, the rock with no value, from the mine. Therefore the mine companies stack the waste in worked out places within the mine. These parts are then walled off with dry stone walling.

Timber

A worked out portion of the mine. This vein was discovered by following a string from Milburn's level. This part of the working was abandoned in 1862. The staging is beinning to sag and rot. On the left is the side or cheek of the vein.

The main levels in mines, where they needed support, were arched in stone, but many side levels and working areas had timber props. In the often damp air of the mines, timber could rot very fast. It was the timberman's job to keep the timbered parts of the mine open and accessible where necessary. The timbermen also saw to the timber platforms constructed at intervals in the rises, and the brattices and ladders in the rises.

In the working areas of the veins, the miners worked above their heads as far as they could reach. Then a timber platform was put in by the timbermen for the men to stand on. As the miners worked upwards and forwards they dropped the waste rock onto these platforms. Piles of deads were stacked and left on the staging.

Although there are trees at Killhope today, these are recent, and anyway would be of little use down the mine. In 1878 the hillsides round Killhope were completely bare of trees, and timber for the mines had to be brought in from friendlier climates. Mr. Beaumont, who owned WB Lead, had a very large estate in Allendale – he owned most of the valley. He grew timber for his mines on parts of this estate.

rmen

Setting props quickly and accurately is a skill that comes with long practice.

WILLIAM ENGLISH

William English was the son of Edward English, the stonemason. He was 35 in 1878, and his wife was the local schoolteacher. They lived at Mount Pleasant, a mile from Park Level Mine and just over the road from William's father's house. They christened two of their daughters Beatrice and Florence – unusual names for Weardale children. William was one of the timbermen in the Killhope mine – he had also worked as a storekeeper and in 1881 would be working as a surface labourer. As a timberman he probably worked with a lad to help him. William and the other timbermen were among the "datal" tradesmen in the mine. This means they were paid by the day, and only for the days they worked. Unfortunately we don't know how much they were paid in 1878, as the company records for that year don't tell us. A few years earlier, in 1871, WB Lead was employing the following datal men in their Weardale mines:

51 woodmen (timbermen) 3/- or 3/3d (15p or 16p) per day

3 rail layers 2/11d (14.5p) per day

1 underground labourer foreman 3/4d (16.5p) per day

97 labourers from 1/2d to 3/3d (6p to 16p) per day

21 blowers (lads turning ventilation fans underground) at 1/- (5p) per day

9 millwrights 1/4d to 4/2d (6.5p to 21p) per day

10 enginekeepers 3/- (15p) per day

9 joiners 3/2d to 4/- (16p to 20p) per day

9 blacksmiths 1/8d to 3/6d (8p to 17.5p) per day

4 surface masons

9 underground masons

Men leading stones and materials

40 surface labourers 1/- to 3/- (5p to 15p) per day

2 sawyers 3/6d and 3/- (17.5p and 15p) per day

1 storekeeper at 3/4d (17p) per day

Stoping
– the Heart of the Mine

PETER MILBURN *In 1878 Peter Milburn was an old man for a miner. He was 54 years old, and had worked in Park Level Mine for a quarter of a century. He probably knew every passage and corner and shaft of this mine better than anybody else. He had been one of the four men who had cut the first sod to start the level in January 1853. He had worked in many parts of the mine, doing both deadwork and stoping.*

Peter lived at School House, a third of a mile to the south of the mine, where he had a small farm of just over 7 acres. Like all the farms in the Killhope valley, School House was owned by Mr. Beaumont. Peter was a widower with five children. He was to die the following year – in July 1879. Times had been hard lately – Peter owed Mr. Beaumont £13/10/- (£13.50) back rent when he died. After his death his family saw no future in Weardale, apart from unemployment and poverty. At the end of that year, in the company of about 50 others from the top of Weardale, they caught the train to London. From there they sailed in the "Margaret Galbraith", an emigrant ship, to start a new life in New Zealand.

School House eventually fell derelict.

In recent years it has been completely rebuilt as a shooting lodge.

We have met some of the tradesmen in the mine, and others doing non-productive work. But the heart of the mine was in the stopes – the working areas in the veins.

Miners took a very keen interest in the vein, its appearance and likely production. Their livelihood depended on it. Many fireside discussions took place in the evening where the prospects were sketched out on the hearthstone in chalk, and fiercely argued over.

Peter Milburn 4 prs agree to raise ore as directed in their ground at 44/– per bing. Subsistence etc.

Peter Milburn, Thos Peart, Joseph Peart, Joseph Baty.

The higher price of lead over the last few years has encouraged Stephen Watson, under agent for WB Lead in charge of Killhope mine, to reopen the abandoned workings in this vein in the hope that it is once again "wageable", and so will repay the cost of working. His hunch, based on years of experience, has paid off; Peter Milburn's partnership of four miners have found a reasonable body of ore. They are pushing the work forward as fast as they can. This is their chance to make good money.

Occasionally the charge of gunpowder explodes unexpectedly – perhaps as you are ramming the hole full, or, when withdrawing the pricker it touches rock and sets up a spark. This was called "firing a shot in the hand", and was a common cause of mine accidents. Men could lose an eye, or a hand. Occasionally miners were killed. For Peter, Joseph and all the other men at Killhope the memory of young Thomas Harrison was very fresh. On the 15th March he had fired a shot in his hand, which had killed him. He was only 18 years old.

...STOPING

– THE HEART OF THE MINE...

Joseph Baty, Thomas Peart, Joseph Peart

These three partners of Peter Milburn's were almost certainly, like Peter, born and brought up in the Killhope valley. Joseph Batey lived and farmed at Far House, one of the last houses in the valley, and one of the highest in England at 1640 feet (520 metres) above sea level. He was 31 years old. The census tells us that Thomas and Joseph Peart, brothers, lived at Cleugh Head, near Far House. They were 31 and 26 in 1878.

Many workings were barely "wageable" – that is to say the amount of ore won from them would barely repay the subsistence money of 15/- (62.5p) per week advanced to the miners.

Leadminers worked by candlelight. Sometimes by the smelly, smoky light of a tallow candle – more often by this time by the better flame from modern composite candles. Quite often the air in the mine was too poor for the candle to burn properly. It had to be laid on its side so the fat ran down to the flame.

Miners had to buy all their own candles, as well as their gunpowder and tools.

Soft veins can be hacked out by pick alone. Harder veins have to be blasted. Thos. Peart and Joseph Peart work together. Working with the easy rhythm of men who have done this job together for years, they are engaged in the tedious task of drilling shot holes in the vein rock. Thomas holds the chisel (the "jumper"). Joseph hits the end of the jumper with a hammer. After each bat with the hammer, Thomas turns the jumper a little in the hole to stop it sticking. And so they work on in the dim flickering candlelight, sometimes hour after hour in very hard rock. Occasionally they stop to clean out the hole with a scraper, or to pour water into it to keep the dust down and make the drilling easier. When the hole is deep enough (about two feet or 60 centimetres), they clean it out again, and, with a long specially shaped spoon, introduce – carefully – a charge of gunpowder to the bottom of the hole. Next one of them puts a long thin needle (the "pricker") into the hole and down to the gunpowder. Round the needle they ram clay or shale to fill the hole up. Finally – and very carefully – one of them pulls the pricker out, and, through the small hole left to the gunpowder by the pricker, puts in a fuse. The charge is now ready for firing. When several shot holes are ready like this, the fuses are lit, the gunpowder explodes, and the rock is broken and brought down. Joseph, Thomas and the others can then shovel up the fallen rock, and hack down any loose and dangerous rock left behind. The whole slow business then begins again.

...Stoping
– The Heart of the Mine

Veins vary hugely in width from 2 – 3 feet (60 – 90 centimetres) up to 12 feet (3.6 metres) or more. The sides of the veins (the "cheeks") are smooth and regular. They lean slightly to one side – the angle from the vertical is the "hade" of the vein, and the sides are the "footwall" and the "hanging wall".

Between the walls is not solid lead ore (galena). The vein might be filled with soft fluorspar, easy to work, with ribs of galena in it, or with hard jumbled up cemented together rocks and minerals with flecks of galena. The variety can be huge, but nearly always lead ore only makes up a small part of the vein – often in bands or ribs an inch or two wide. Solid masses of galena are very rare.

A partnership of miners was given a standard length in the vein to work – usually 10 fathoms (60 feet or 18.3 metres). This was their "ground".

First they drove the level forward along the vein. Then they hacked out the roof as high above their heads

Gunpowder or other explosive or inflammable substance shall only be used underground in the mine as follows:
a) it shall not be stored in the mine
b) it shall not be taken into the mine, except in a case or canister containing not more than 4lb.
c) a workman shall not have in use at one time in any one place more than one of such cases or canisters.

Metalliferous Mines
Regulation Act 1872

Previously it was the custom to store whole wooden casks of gunpowder in the mine. By 1878 dynamite was beginning to be used widely in place of gunpowder. 4lb of gunpowder is about 1.8 kilos.

as they could reach. Heavy round timbers were wedged across the vein, and planks laid on these to form a higher floor for working off. This floor also acted as a roof to the level. Standing on the platform, miners cut away at the vein above them, working upwards and forwards, dropping the broken rock down onto the timber. This ever-increasing pile of rock beneath their feet meant that the men could always reach the roof above them. The bouse – the veinstuff with ore in it – was tipped into hoppers leading down to the level below. From the hoppers it was dropped into horse drawn tubs, or waggons, and led out of the mine into the bouse teems for separation on the washing rake.

The Black Spit

Men working in the most distant parts of Park Level Mine suffered greatly from bad air. Sometimes they couldn't get to their workplace at all.

Fatal accidents were much less common. One death at Killhope was recorded by a local historian:

"Both tragic and miraculous was an accident that occurred to two miners in Killhope mine in 1864. Thomas Rowell and Graham Peart were working high up in a rise when a sudden heavy fall carried Peart down to his death. Rowell was sitting on his "honkers" on the side and though struck was able to maintain his position. The moans of his mate coming up from below soon ceased, then in Stygian darkness the crashing of stones flying past him was the only sound he heard for three days and nights. He kept himself alive by eating his tallow candles and catching falling drops of water."

(Weardale Memories and Traditions, by John Lee.)

Samples of the air of mines in the north of England were analysed by Dr. Smith, in 110 instances, and the air was found to be:
- *pure or nearly so in 14 or 12.72%,*
- *decidedly impure in 27 or 24.52%, and*
- *extremely bad in 69 or 62.72%.*

Leadminers waged a constant war with two main enemies – too much water and not enough air.

Lead mines were very poorly ventilated, particularly in the further reaches of the mine. Yet men had to work in places where a candle would hardly burn.

As a result bad air, full of dust and gunpowder reek, killed the miners slowly but surely.

After a very few years down the mine, men began hockling up black mucus from their lungs. This was called the black spit; the first sign of the lung disease which would first cripple and then kill them.

At what age do men usually discontinue working from inability to bear the fatigue of work? It is not in my power to state an average, but some are obliged to give up work before 40; some work till 45, and some till 50. Do many attain the age at which they become entitled to pensions, namely 65? I am afraid not... Is it a rare thing for men to get above 40 without being touched in their lungs permanently? Very rare indeed; I cannot call to mind having met with a miner who is not more or less affected with shortness of breathing before he is 40 years of age. Permanent shortness of breathing? Yes. At what age do you consider a miner an old man? I should consider a miner really an old man between 55 and 60. A decidedly older man than an ordinary workman? Yes.

William Ewart was surgeon to the London Lead Company. He gave evidence to the Kinnaird Commission in 1862.

Sometimes tunnels and shafts are driven to connect workings in different parts of the mine simply to help the flow of air round the mine. This ventilation door has been installed to regulate and direct the air flow into parts of the mine where it is difficult to breathe.

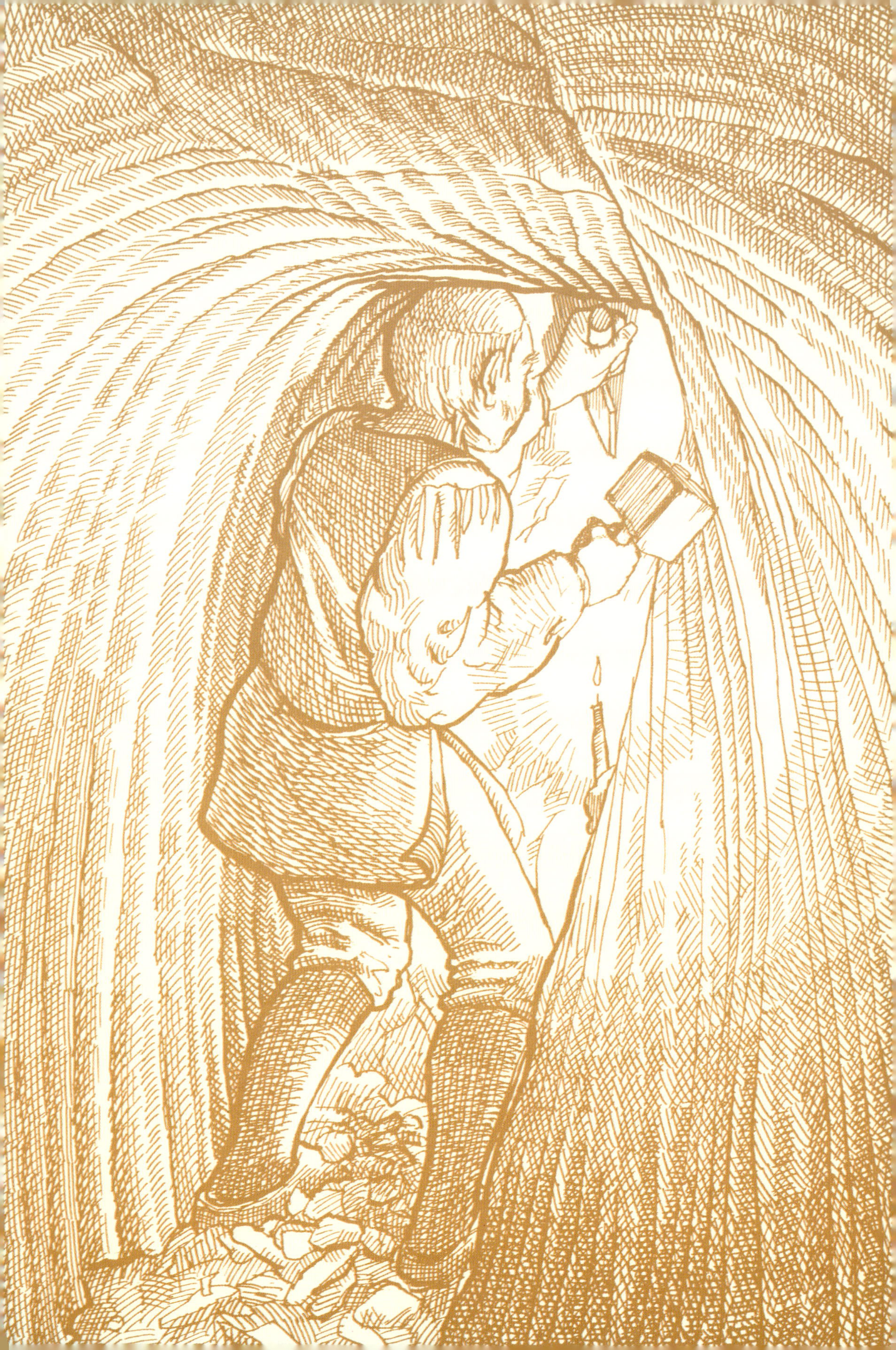

The Old Man

The old man has been a constant source of both admiration and exasperation for miners of every generation. The old man is the miner's name for both the holes left by centuries of mining activity, and for the long forgotten people who made them.

Although from the 1840's onwards WB Lead insisted on detailed and very accurate plans and sections being kept of all the workings, older plans were very crude and simple, and the workings of two or three hundred years before that were long forgotten.

Killhope's veins had been worked for at least 200 years before 1878; lead may well have been mined here since the Middle Ages. Peter Milburn and his fellow miners must often have felt that wherever they went in Park Level Mine the 'old man' had beaten them to the best bits of the vein. Uncertainty was everywhere.

"28 May 1861 Park Level. Peter Milburn 6 men rising in Old Moss vein from east side of level roof ...probably the vein will be good if the old man has not wrought it before."

"1868 2 Peter Milburn and boy searching old ground in MIddle Grove vein... has not made wages this past quarter but is getting west to where the old man seems to have left of(f) or nearly so..."

"1869 6 Francis Peart searching old ground in Level Grove vein ...this ground ...seems to have been extensively wrought."

...THE OLD MAN

Consequently it was not unknown for miners to break through into the old man – unsuspected and long abandoned workings. If these were full of water they could be a hazard. Miners, full of optimism, opened up what they thought were new areas of vein only to find that the old man had been there before them and had "slit out" the best parts.

Gunpowder for blasting rock came into mining in the second half of the 17th century, and into widespread use in the 18th century. Before that, all driving of tunnels and sinking of shafts could only be done with hand tools. Old man's levels were narrow and twisting as they followed lines of weakness in the rock. They were only just wide and high enough for a man to squeeze through. You can see the score marks of the chisels down the walls as each inch was painstakingly chipped out.

The old man's level could date from Elizabethan times, or even earlier. Nobody knows for sure. In following lines of weakness through the rock the old man missed – by just a few feet – the vein which Peter Milburn and his partners are now working. Sometimes the old man built fires against the rock face and then dashed water against the hot rock. Sudden cooling weakened and shattererd the rock.

Hymer's Level was driven along a weak vein with traces of lead ore. The fault has thrown down the sandstone which forms one cheek of the vein. However the other side of the vein is in unstable crumbly shale which needs a lot of timber support to keep the roof and sides secure. The tunnel has collapsed just past the old man's level.

Managing
the Mine

By 1878 Park Level Mine had been working for 25 years and many parts of the mine had been explored, developed, worked and abandoned.

Although the men, with their bargain system, kept the illusion of being free agents negotiating with the mine agent about where to work and for how much, by this time management of the mine was very much stricter. The men were told what to do.

Stephen Watson was the Inspector of Mines – the underagent in charge of Park Level Mine. He reported to J. C. Cain, chief Weardale agent for Mr. Beaumont. WB Lead in Weardale was divided into three districts, each with an agent in charge. The agent made weekly visits round the workings, making notes for Mr. Cain. He checked that the men were working neatly and tidily and keeping in the vein. He checked that rises were being driven to a true vertical, levels along a correct and straight line, and that the timbering and arching were all in satisfactory condition.

A waterblast is a very simple but extremely effective way of blowing air into distant parts of the mine. Water is dropped down a pipe from the surface; it pulls air in with it. At the bottom of the shaft the precious air is trapped in a box, and piped through the mine to where men are working. The water flows out along the level.

Water and A

Air ←

Water ←

...Managing the mine

He made sure men didn't just dump their waste rock where it suited them; for their rubbish might get in the way of future work. All waste rock had to be stowed neatly in worked out parts of the mine. He reported on the value and prospects of each part of this rambling mine.

Watson and Cain decided which parts of the mine to develop; where men were to work; where "dead work" or exploration was to take place. In 1878 was it worth setting on a couple of men to clear through the collapse in Hymer's Level and explore further along the vein to see if there was a payable orebody? Was it worth rising up from the level into the strata above or sinking a shaft below to try the vein higher up or lower down? Dead work like this was expensive, but if Park Level Mine was to have a future, then new reserves of ore had to be found to be worked when the known deposits of galena were mined out.

"Killhope, 5 December 1878.

2 Wm English's ground. All the levels drifts rises and climbing ways are in good condition except the west end air drift which wants repairing though it is all open yet".

Stephen Watson recording in his notebook the work of William English, timberman.

STEPHEN WATSON INSPECTOR OF MINES Stephen Watson did not live in the Killhope valley, but a few miles down the dale in Ireshopeburn. By 1878 he was spending nearly all his working week managing the very large and complicated mine that Killhope had become. Like Peter Milburn he knew the mine inside out. A number of his working notebooks survive and they tell us a great deal about how Park Level Mine was run. He earned rather more than the average miner, but his was still not a princely income at £100 a year.

Park Level

From Hymer's Vein, Park Level continues in a dead straight line for half a mile crossing several more veins, each of which was worked in turn. Then the tunnel changes direction, following the line of one vein – Trent Vein – towards Killhopehead vein. This far vein is nearly a mile from the entrance to the mine, and it took the miners twenty years of continuous toil to hack out the level this far. Only the biggest companies, like WB Lead, could afford the kind of investment needed for large projects like this.

Driving through some of the hard limestones could be a nightmare, with progress measured in inches a week.

The 1871 census shows us that just about every man and boy of working age in the valleys of Killhope and Wellhope at the top of Weardale worked in the lead mines. Joseph Graham, featured in the exhibition in the visitor centre, was a leadminer before he left for America in 1852. Five of his six brothers were leadminers – the sixth became a shoemaker. His four sisters all married leadminers. As we have seen, the term leadminer covered a whole range of jobs.

Boys worked on the surface, on the washing rake or at the mill. In the winter, when washing was impossible, older boys came into the mine to start learning the trade and skills of their fathers.

Today the tunnel of Park Level is quiet, apart from the splashing of visitors' feet through the water. In 1878 it was a busy thoroughfare. Horse drawn tubs pulled the ore and waste rock from the mine. Others carried back in stone for arching, timber for the woodmen, rails and sleepers for the rail layers.

At intervals the level has been widened out to allow a passing place, or room for horses to turn round. A couple of tubs can be kept here.

No boy under the age of 12 years, and no girl or woman of any age, shall be employed in or allowed to be for the purpose of employment in any mine to which this Act applies below ground.

Metalliferous Mines Regulation Act 1872

All mine companies chose carefully the best places from which to start their main levels, to get the easiest working. The well chosen situation of Park Level is ideal, for the tunnel is driven in soft shale, but just beneath a much harder rock – sandstone. The sandstone forms a good strong roof for the level, whilst the shale is easier to dig out. There are no timber supports at all in this part of the mine. A row of stepping stones along beside the rail track is a very unusual feature here – the miners are doing all they can to stop their feet getting wet.

The Engine Chamber

The engine keeper had to keep the wheel and pumps in running order, greasing the bearings and moving parts regularly. He would have had more than one mine to look after

We have seen how the problem of lack of air in the mine could be tackled, and how it helped cause an early death for so many men.

The other enemy – water – wasn't life threatening in the same way. The problem was how to control it. If harnessed, water could be put to good use.

As soon as miners started sinking shafts below the lowest level in any mine they ran into water. The amount of water could vary hugely from place to place. If there wasn't too much it could be lifted out in buckets by a lad winding a handroller at the top of the shaft. When a shaft was being sunk it could very often be kept dewatered in this way. However a more permanent solution was to install pumps to draw water from the mine. These were cast iron pipes with a plunger working within them. Sometimes mine water was so acid that wooden pumps had to be used; iron was eaten away. Pumps had to be powered – occasionally this too was done by hand, like the old fashioned village pump.

THOMAS GRAHAM, LEADMINER *Thomas was born and brought up at Hill Top, one of the small farms perched on the hillside further up the valley from Park Level Mine. He had four older sisters – all of whom married leadminers – and six younger brothers. All but one of the brothers were leadminers.*

Thomas was 56 in 1878, widowed with eight children of his own. He lived at Burnt Hills, near many of his relatives. Earlier in the year he had been a leader of a partnership of miners, a skilled and highly experienced miner himself. But he was not offered work when new bargains were let in August, so his mining days were over.

In company with many others he saw no future in a depressed Weardale, and sailed on the "Margaret Galbraith" to New Zealand the following year. This was a bold step for a man of his age; we can only hope he prospered.

Next year, 1879, an enginekeeper at Old Gin Wheel, Allenheads, disobeying "strict instructions" will try to oil the bearings of a wheel without stopping it first.

"Sep 18th. A man named Thomas Heslop was killed in a mine at Allenheads by getting entangled in a waterwheel. He was completely torn to pieces, and some parts of his remains were washed out at the level mouth."

...THE ENGINE CHAMBER